Lorraine,

Together we will change the world.

Thank you!

Sage Lewis

Out of the Shadows

Out of the Shadows

An American Homeless Story
by Sage & Rocky Lewis

The photo on the back cover of Sage and Rocky was taken by Scott R. Galvin and reproduced with his permission.

The photo of Sage inside the book was taken by Isaac Reese at Institute for Justice and was reproduced with their permission.

The photo of Emerald Village was purchased on IStock Photo on November 3, 2018.

All other photos were taken by Sage Lewis.

Dedication

This book is dedicated to the true heroes of America: The countless people of America who quietly take extreme actions to make the world a better place for those most in need.

At print time, the City of Akron had ordered we remove the tents. We debated editing the book, to place our mention of tents in the village to past tense, but we did not. Our community is so strong, even without the tents.

Our current and former residents and many volunteers come regularly to the Day Center, support us out in the field, in social media and in person. They can take down the tents, but they can never dismantle the community and heartfelt spirit created here.

The world is filled with incredibly kind, generous and giving beings.

You give us faith in humanity.

We will never be able to thank you enough.

With love,
Sage & Rocky

Introduction

A lot of emergency vehicles show up to an overdose. I never know what I'm going to walk into when I come to work. But when 3 cop cars, two fire trucks and an ambulance are sitting in front of your building, you have to imagine it's not going to be a normal day.

We've had two opiate overdoses at our homeless village. In both cases, the person lived. Each time the person was saved this way: someone walked by their tent, noticed and heard something unusual, and then looked inside to find the person barely breathing and slumped over.

At this point, everyone rallies. The person who discovered the victim calls for a member of the on-site, homeless-run security team. The security member calls 911 and administers the Narcan they carry. And the homeless overdose victim survives even though the odds are against them. Experiencing homelessness while being an opioid addict makes a person nine times more likely to die than if they were stably housed.[1]

Our village in winter.
The Homeless are survivalists.

While we have fantasies of communities as places with tree lined streets and picket fences, these people, in mismatched tents on donated crushed asphalt, are a community. Everyone here is united under the umbrella of newfound purpose and dignity. This is what community is really about. Checking in on your neighbor. Caring about one another. Working together to move from surviving to thriving.

Our village is made up of an average of 45 people, although we almost always have a waiting list of 20 or more people desperate for a tent and a place to call home. You can typically see our caring community in action in any given afternoon.

I've had a woman give me her very last dollar to help pay the electric bill for the facility. Another member of our community spent his entire food stamp money for the month on ribs, potatoes and corn to cook a feast for every resident.

People here watch out for 79 year old John to make sure he is get-

This is Brandon. He single-handedly built that fence behind him. He now has a home, wife and baby.

ting into his tent without falling, making it to the bathroom and eating regularly. And many gather to help Alice as she deals with her cancer surgeries.

People here find purpose in giving back to the tent community. The residents volunteer to run our security, laundry, clothing, kitchen and administrative departments. While only an hour a day is required for ongoing residency, most work full time, 7 days a week. They choose to do it. They know what we all know -- being useful and needed is life's gift. They crave what we all crave -- to contribute and be respected for our contributions.

While this story is set in a tent village created and run by local homeless people, it is actually the story of what it means to be human.

How many of us would never know if our neighbor had a medical emergency? While we once sat on our porches while children roamed the neighborhoods, we now sit on our back decks while children play alone inside.

This is "Bama" and his dog Nomad. They currently live alone in the woods. Dogs often are incredibly important to homeless people.

Is this simply happening to us or is this what we want? Regardless, we just keep plodding down this path of growing increasingly isolated as we stare at our personal glowing devices. Yet we need each other to survive.

 "We have created a Star Wars civilization, with Stone Age emotions." So says, Edward O. Wilson of Harvard University, eminent biologist and two time Pulitzer Prize winner. In his book, *The Social Conquest of Earth*, he declares that humans are best served living in communities that share labor and behave altruistically.[2]

Wilson studied ant colonies in the rain forest to determine and verify his theories on humanity's communal nature. But our tent village is a study of its own and has shown me how community is not a luxury, but a very basic human need. There is very little "Star Wars civilization" for the extreme low income homeless population. Most in our village live on less than $1 a day.

As you read this book -- with facts and stories about homelessness

These are villagers and supporters waiting for a city council meeting to begin.

and our homeless community -- I hope that you may see yourself in some of these pages, so you will understand the homeless of America a little better. It is only through understanding our country's most vulnerable people that we will be able to help them reintegrate back into society. We must become a supportive community that welcomes them back into the fold.

Until that happens, we must allow them to form their own smaller communities where they can find safety, dignity and purpose. Who knows… as we share the story of our small community, you may even feel a bit of envy for these people. It's not a utopia by any means, but even these folks who have nothing by today's standards, have gained so much by living in this small tent village. By losing everything they have stripped away much of the unnecessary and stumbled upon connection and community. They have rekindled the glowing ember of what it means to be human.

   -   Sage Lewis

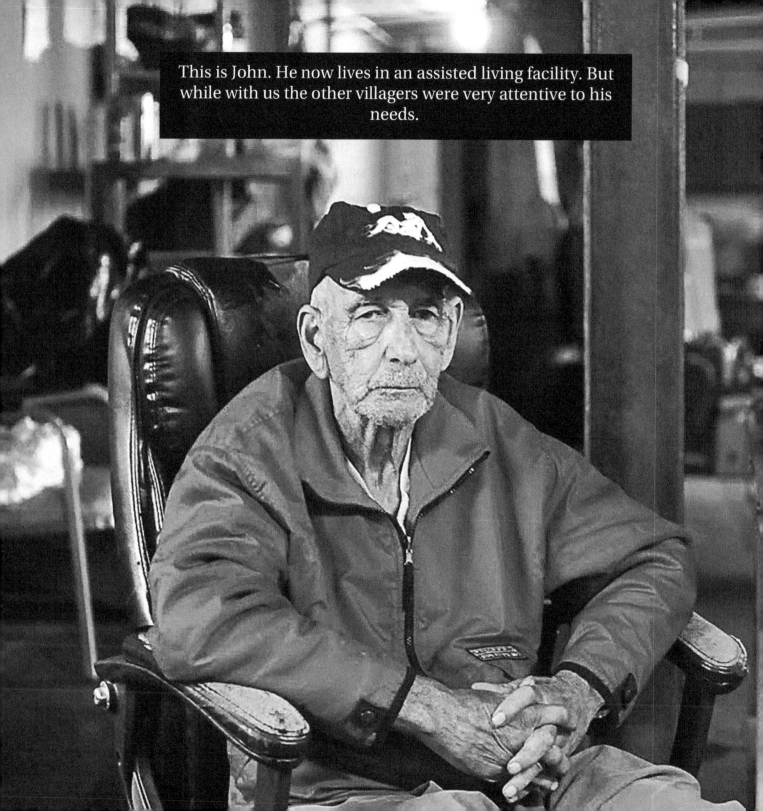

This is John. He now lives in an assisted living facility. But while with us the other villagers were very attentive to his needs.

Homelessness is a Choice

How does a person become homeless? Sometimes people say, "Homelessness is a choice." Meaning, we suppose, that those on the street are choosing that life because [insert reason: to do drugs, not work, etc].

What the housed are really saying is that homeless people have made a series of poor choices leading to life on the street and the homeless are not interested in changing those choices.

This is a common argument heard even from government officials. If a city has houses or apartments, on a list somewhere, declared as available, then anyone they see on the street must have chosen to be there.

On the surface this makes sense and may even be occasionally true. What makes a person homeless *can* be a series of bad choices. But, stereotypes don't stand up well to the nuanced reality facing home-

This is Patty. She has been homeless for many years. She tries for housing, but it often doesn't work out.

less individuals. Each situation is different.

Unfortunately, the people in the housing systems, those in need and those who serve, can find the system they are within limiting and difficult to manage. Layers of complexity await people looking for assistance with housing, food, transportation, mental health and addiction needs. And these are often the same folks that found daily life in society overwhelming for a variety of reasons.

Does this mean they are weak at their core? That they are unworthy of society's help? That they are unredeemable, have nothing to offer and belong in our alleys unseen?

Homelessness in America today is one of these rationalized falsehoods. Digging deep, one must ask, "What is the moral justification for allowing anyone, drug user, mentally ill, disabled or otherwise, to lie unprotected and vulnerable in the cold, harsh streets? Does their life have so little value?"

Considering the wealth in our country, with over $500 billion a year

This is Gary on the first day he ever voted.

spent on defense alone, and waste like $5 million spent on hand-blown crystal wine glasses for U.S. embassies, common people may rightly think Americans living on our streets is an unacceptable reality.

After all, it is not an impossible problem. We are talking about 500,000 people in need out of 325 million or so people. We seem to know how to house people in other situations. Since 1980, the U.S. has taken in, and housed, 3 million refugees.[3] So we know how to house about 70,000 people coming to the U.S. each and every year. It would seem, with a number like 500,000 homeless people, we may be able to address the issue productively within a decade. Are we simply choosing not to address the issue in earnest?

We believe this negligence may, in part, be connected to our biases against the homeless -- our inherently American distaste for those not working or contributing the way we feel they should.

We hope to tackle many of these biases in the following pages, by answering some common questions people have about the homeless and by highlighting some members of our community just as they are -- human and therefore flawed, and, yet, hopeful even while houseless.

This is Randy. He's stayed with us. But he mostly feels more comfortable in the woods alone.

This is Herman. He has been fundamentally important to keeping our facility running smoothly.

Herman

Herman is 66 years old. One could say Herman has chosen to be homeless at different times of his life. After all, he hitchhiked to different parts of the U.S. and once took off to California in a VW with his sister and a few buddies. He laughs remembering: "That car blew up in Phoenix."

There have been a series of interesting jobs in Herman's life in different locations -- a casino worker in Arizona and Vegas, an industrial job in California, a full time Walmart job in Ohio and smaller patches on work in between in Texas, Florida, Colorado and Washington state.

Herman says, "I was always an adventurer. I'd run out of money and move spur of the moment. I've been homeless off and on during my travels. I once camped out on the Colorado River for a couple months. Camped out in Washington state for a bit. Went

Eva comes every Tuesday to feed our community homemade food. They consider her family.

back to Bullhead City Arizona to live with my Mom for a while. She thought I was dead. Then I dated a girl in Texas and lived there for five years."

But it wasn't until Herman got back to Ohio in his 60s that he became what he would call "really homeless." He had a full time job making $48,000 a year, but found it was not paying the bills his then girlfriend was accruing.

"She liked to borrow money. I kept overdrawing the bank account unexpectedly. Then I injured myself on the job. Even walking became difficult. Our place was in her name. She had the car in her name too."

A fight with his girlfriend led to Herman being driven to Akron and dropped off. That's when he started sleeping under a bridge. He got attacked on the street while sleeping by a guy wielding a hammer.

"Then I came here. It's been an eye opening experience."

Herman at work. He has a home now, and has retired, but volunteers full time at the Day Center.

Tent city gave Herman some of the stability he needed to gain control back over his bank account that his girlfriend was draining. It took him 4 months to get everything back in order. He remembers that one of the first things the folks at tent city did was get him a walking cane. Then he was able to find a doctor, get to appointments and start recovering from his work injury.

Now people at the village look to Herman as a father figure. Herman has been voted into tri-council, a tent village government position, at every village election by a landslide.

"They look to me for guidance. You gotta be stern, strong-minded and strong-willed here. I try and treat everyone fairly. I let them speak their peace and then I speak my opinion. I am a firm person, but they need that. Sometimes you need hard love. Gotta dish it out every once in a while."

Herman has a place now, but still volunteers full time at the onsite day center and continues to hold his elected tri-council position. He's says things are "looking good." He is in AA, living within his income and seeing doctors for his COPD and arthritis.

"I appreciate this place. And all that's been done for me. And the friends that I've made here. I'm like everybody's father here, and I have been entrusted with so much. It's been an uplifting experience."

This is Amie, Trae, Ducky and Herman. This was taken at an on-site Christmas party.

Steve, once homeless, is a hard worker. He saved, bought a minivan, and now drives homeless to appointments.

Why Don't They Stay With Family?

On any given day, there are just shy of half a million foster children in the United States.[4] In the latest report from the U.S. Department of Health and Human Services, Administration for Children and Families, Ohio had 177,368 total referrals for child abuse and neglect. Of those, 80,762 reports were referred for investigation.[5] In 2016, nine of every 1,000 children in Ohio were abused or neglected.[6]

The tent village in Akron, Ohio, is filled with once abused children and children from the foster care system. For them, staying with family is not an option due to abuse, neglect or nonexistence. When family does exist and is available, it is not typically a never ending resource. Homeless people are homeless for a reason. Most commonly those reasons include mental health problems, addiction, learning or health disabilities and criminal records.

This is George. Before staying with us he lived under a bush. He needs assisted living, urgently, but the lists are incredibly long, so we care for him.

For example, we have had several autistic and intellectually disabled adults living in tent village whose parents could no longer support them after they reached adulthood. We have had an elderly man with dementia whose child was unable to care for him. We once had a woman with a severe intellectual disability, who showed up at our doorstep without the capability to even share her diagnosis. And we receive countless drug addicts at our day center seeking food, laundry service and showers. They live on the street because their family had to enforce tough love or risk the health and safety of themselves and other family members.

Many older homeless come to tent village and the day center after an elderly parent passes. It's a common story of an adult child, with siblings, who lives with an ailing parent. The siblings see the adult child as someone who has failed to launch. The adult child believes they help care for their older parent. When the parent dies, the story is the same all over America. The siblings evict the adult child living with the elderly and let them know the free ride has ended. In this case, family was taking care of a likely homeless person for years, but they are no longer willing or able.

So what is the answer? Do we, as a society, have an obligation to care for those neglected or separated from their family support systems? Many say no. Others say it is the job of the government. Others still believe it is the role of philanthropists to rise to this occasion.

The Homeless Charity has heard the call to step in and do what we can for the invisible and alone. Humans should have basic rights to things like safety, food and shelter. We are doing what we can to ensure those needs are met.

Villagers pose with these high school girls who routinely travel the world helping those in need. They brought dinner and cleaned up a remote camp site.

Donnie always thought she'd be taken care of by her husband and live in the house she owned free and clear.

Donnie

Donnie is a good example of a homeless person who cannot stay with family. Donnie has a mother, a sister and two children who love her dearly, but she cannot stay with any of them. She's been homeless for 4 months now.

"My Mother stays in an AMHA apartment, so I can't stay with her because it's against the rules and she'll end up homeless. My sister let me stay for a while, but she's helping out my grown children and I'd rather she help them than me. I can't over tax her. My daughter works full time and lives with her until she makes enough to get her own place. My son lives with a few of his friends while they all work to save up for their own places. I can't stay with him either. I don't want to add to either of their burdens. I have signed up for AMHA and I just hope that comes through."

Some might ask, "Did Donnie not plan, not know, she would need a place of her own before she became homeless?" Some homeless

Long-time supporter, Eva Buhite, serving one of her Tuesday lunches.

people see their fate coming down the pipeline. They live paycheck to paycheck, miss bills, dodge collectors, but it was never that way for Donnie. She was a stay at home mom in a working class family and thought she'd always be taken care of by her husband. But her husband and father of her children, who had a good job and a good pension at Goodyear Tire and Rubber Company, died unexpectedly. And he and Donnie hadn't saved or planned for his death.

Together, they owned a home in Norton and had moved from Akron to Norton so their kids could go to a better school.

"We used all our savings to buy that house in Norton and we paid it off. We were so proud of that. When my husband died, he thought I'd be getting his Goodyear pension, but I was too young, so they gave me a one-time payout. I was grieving, and I had never had responsibilities like this, and I didn't know I was supposed to fight for something different. I just said, 'okay.'"

Donnie's money management of the small lump sum only lasted so long. Bills, funeral and medical expenses, money spent on the kids,

This is a homeless man living in the woods in the winter. He was forced to move by a man threatening him with a baseball bat.

and home repairs soon left Donnie with too little and she fell behind on property taxes. It took a while, but eventually, they boarded up the house she and her husband owned outright.

Donnie says, "I tried to hold out in the boarded up house. The kids had grown and moved out, and I lived there alone as long as I could. Then I met a man who wasn't a nice person and he moved into the house too. When I went to stay with a friend at Thanksgiving, she wouldn't let me go back to the old house because that abusive man was there too."

Donnie stayed with her friend in Doylestown for as long as she could, but eventually her friend ran into money trouble and got evicted. Donnie didn't know her friend's financial situation was as bad as it was and found herself instantly on the street with only what she could carry.

"I had a few friends, but you find out who your friends are quick when you come to their door."

Villagers and volunteers are holding hand-made quilts made for the villagers. They made over 50 quilts.

Donnie found a new identity that night. She was no longer just staying with friends, avoiding her abusive boyfriend, or managing being a down and out widow. She was now a homeless woman.

"The first night, I cried a lot and walked the street all night. I hid what I had under the bushes, but everything eventually got stolen piece by piece. Finally, I just gave everything away to someone who gave me a few nights on their couch. I'm 52 and have had back surgery, so I couldn't carry it anyway."

The worst part for Donnie is feeling like she failed her kids and has no control over her future. But she knew she wasn't the only one who had fallen on hard times. She saw several people in her neighborhood lose their houses, which sat empty and boarded up for years. Even before her own house was boarded up, she wished people could live in those structures.

"So many good people lose everything. Why couldn't they stay in those houses? People still aren't in them. They say you're just two paychecks away from being homeless. It's so true. Two paychecks and you're on the street."

Donnie was on the street for a few weeks, doing what she could to get by, and people kept telling her about a tent village in Akron.

When she finally got to 15 Broad Street, she was so nervous she walked right by the building. The next time she walked by, a friendly member asked her if she wanted to come in and get a cup of coffee.

"I've been here ever since," says Donnie. "It's a blessing to be here and I love it. I mean, I don't like living in a tent, the porta potties are gross, and it gets cold at night, but I like that we're helping other people. Even though I am homeless, I can still lend a hand to others."

Donnie recalled a man she had helped the previous week. "You think you're at your lowest and then you see people worse off. Just last week, I saw someone getting soaked out front with all their belongings, so I got them some dry blankets and a garbage bag.

Like the Bible says, 'when you're doing for the least of mine, you're doing it for me.'"

This is Mikey the woodchuck. He is a supporter of our community garden.

This is our computer lab in the Day Center. We currently have about 8 workstations and wifi. All is run by villagers.

Why Don't They Stay in Shelters?

A religious member at tent village tells of his experience at a local, privately run shelter: "I had to go to church three times a day there -- before breakfast, dinner and bed. If I refused, I was back on the street. I love Jesus and church, but that's just too much even for me. And it was lights out at 8pm. Like we were kids. What adult goes to sleep at eight o'clock? And I never knew when I gave up my things, if I would get them all back. People had their stuff go missing all the time."

Shelters are problematic because people would rather live on the street than live in the shelter. That alone should raise some eyebrows that the American shelter system is dysfunctional.

Common reported issues of shelters include things like:
- ☐ Not being able to store your things safely.
- ☐ Having to leave most of your things behind in order to spend one night in a shelter.

Our tent village at max occupancy. We had 45 tents and 50 villagers.

- ☐ Feeling unsafe because of drug use.
- ☐ Being required to attend church services and pray before receiving services.
- ☐ Adhering to extremely early curfews.
- ☐ Being unable to stay for more than several days in a row.
- ☐ Waiting lists.
- ☐ Not being able to stay with your mate.
- ☐ Not being able to keep your pet.

When shelters are unavailable, and when available are operated like jails, it is problematic. People feel they lose their humanity and their rights when entering a shelter and that should warrant consideration, especially if we want people to choose a shelter bed over a tarp and a park bench. And it's not just a few bad apples. These are common experiences across the country regarding homeless shelters.[7] But it's not just draconian rules or forced religion that keep people away.

There are also a lack of beds, meaning one must stand in line each day to get a place. There are very few shelters that allow couples to

This is Harold at an Akron Art Museum fundraiser. We reconstructed his home for people to experience.

remain together as most are for women only or for men only. Almost none offer storage for belongings larger than a backpack and those forced to sleep on the street treasure items like sleeping bags and pillows, so waiting in a shelter line means stashing their things under bushes and bridges hoping they're still there the next day.

Perhaps, most importantly, these shelters are for nighttime sleeping only. There is nowhere to rest your head during the day, which means if you're sick, work at night or have disabilities, the street and a spot under a bush or bridge makes more "sense" than a shelter. Especially if the shelter has monthly stay limits and many do.

In many ways these conditions exist, not because shelters are poorly designed, but because they were designed for a different purpose than transitional life between the street and an apartment. They were designed to be emergency shelters for a few days or weeks, not longer term alternatives to affordable housing.

And we need affordable housing so that less people face eviction and life on the street. There is not a single county in America that

This is a remote campsite that was ordered to be taken down very near the same time our village was ordered to come down.

NOTICE

PERSONAL PROPERTY LOCATED AT THIS SITE CONSTITUTES AN ILLEGAL ENCAMPMENT ON CITY PROPERTY. THE CITY OF AKRON WILL REMOVE PERSONAL PROPERTY FROM THIS ENCAMPMENT ON 10/15/18

THE CITY WILL STORE NON-ABANDONED PROPERTY FOR 30 DAYS FROM THE DATE OF REMOVAL.

YOU MAY RECLAIM NON-ABANDONED PROPERTY AT 850 E. MARKET ST. BY FIRST CALLING 375-2297

YOU MUST PROVIDE A DISCRIPTION OF THE PROPERTY IN ORDER TO RECLAIM IT.

THE CITY WILL DISPOSE OF ALL UNCLAIMED PROPERTY AFTER 30 DAYS IN STORAGE.

can meet its needs of affordable housing for extremely low income residents. As of the latest Census Report, 46 million people live in poverty in the United States.[8]

While we think of this lack of affordable housing as a coastal city issue, that is simply not the case. Extremely low income households face a housing shortage in every state and major metropolitan area. Only 35 affordable and available rental homes exist for every 100 extremely low income renters. The worst case scenario is in Nevada, which has only 15 affordable rentals for every 100 extremely low income renter households. The best case is in Maine, where there are 59 rentals available for every 100 extremely low income renter households.[9]

There are 11.1 million renters in the U.S. that are paying more than 50 percent of their income for housing. This puts all of those Americans at risk of getting evicted, becoming homeless and landing at a shelter with a wait list or a stay limit.[10]

If these people get evicted, where do we expect them to go?

This is Hugh with the key to his new home. He was thrilled.

Hugh Miller

Hugh lived as long as he could at the local shelter, which has stay limits, but he was given an exception because he was part of their job program. Then he was injured on the job, went to get treatment at a local hospital and was sent to physical therapy. But the conditions of remaining at the shelter required actively working, so he was back out on the street.

He lived on the streets until he got a job that could accommodate his work injury. He became a telemarketer and was able to get back into the local shelter. However, he and his girlfriend, who also worked, decided to use the new income to rent a room together instead of staying in the shelter without belongings or the option to be together.

A few months later, Hugh got sick again and went to the hospital with bleeding ulcers. "I was in bad shape and called in, called off for a week for medical reasons, but I got fired anyway."

This are 2 local news trucks in front of our building. They have regularly covered our story.

Soon both Hugh and his girlfriend were homeless yet again. "We wanted to keep our things. We had some suitcases and found out about the tent village online. We came here and you had space available."

Hugh says, "God wants me to be here and do this volunteer work." Hugh was the intake administrator at the village and volunteered full time. "I'm houseless, but I'm not homeless. Even when I get work, I will still volunteer here. I'm here for the people. I'm doing good."

While Hugh is new to homelessness, he is no stranger to poverty. Originally from Arkansas, Hugh lived with his family and worked for 15 years in a chicken and turkey processing plant. When his mother died, Hugh moved to Ohio.

"Before moving from Arkansas to Ohio, I had never been homeless before, but I had always been poor. I never judged the homeless. My clothes have always been from Goodwill and we missed meals

This is Gary at the Food Bank. We go at least once a week to get food for villagers and neighbors.

and had to eat the same thing over and over. I was taught not to judge a book from its cover."

Hugh wants to keep volunteering at the village, but also wants to move on.

"I want to get a job again. I went through an agency to get housing. They let me know I couldn't get housing until I got a job. But I still have medical issues -- ulcers and frozen shoulder and nerve damage in my hand from the chicken plant -- so it's difficult to find work, but I have a lot of applications out. And I might qualify for social security. I'm working on that too."

As of print time, Hugh did get an apartment and was working towards becoming employed again.

This is Sage and Brett taking scrap to a scrap yard. Brett also panhandles. He has a wide array of mental and physical disabilities that make holding a job difficult.

Why Don't They Get Jobs?

While we have all heard a story of a panhandler that refused to follow up on a work lead, the fact is that around 40% of the homeless work either full or part time while they are homeless.[11]

Getting a job without a permanent address, without access to running water or clean clothes, and without transportation is incredibly difficult. Now add in a criminal record, a disability or a mental illness.

Here is a breakdown of the issues we see our tent village residents battling each day that often stand in the way of obtaining gainful employment.

Lack of Affordable or Available Transportation: Bus passes in Akron run about $15 a week. Buses often do not run on routes near available work. Missing a bus means termination of employment and having something as simple as an alarm clock wake you up to get you showered, groomed and to a bus on time can be a monu-

This is Dee who was a villager for some time. She is an astoundingly good singer and guitarist.

mental task for a homeless person.

Lack of Affordable or Available Child Care: Mothers with children find working particularly difficult while homeless. Mothers are often engaged in the full time logistics of having a homeless child to feed, shelter somehow, cloth and educate. We have seen pregnant women be told they must work in order to acquire housing, only to be told by every fast food employer in town to return and apply after the delivery of the baby. But there is nowhere to raise the infant after the delivery let alone anyone to lend a hand while the new mother works.

Physical Disability: Lack of health care to manage a disability, trauma or disease often exacerbates this issue of finding work. An ER will not refuse treatment for a homeless person, but they also will not necessarily refer (or certainly cannot facilitate) needed follow ups with specialists that cost money, require transportation, or ask for documentation the homeless patient might not have on hand.

Consider this simple instruction from an ER doctor: "Go home.

This is Eric and Aimee at a local school fair. They helped people make bags of things to give to other homeless people.

Take this prescription, rest with the injury elevated." Or "Clean the wound 3 times a day and change the bandage...."

To a homeless person these instructions contain a myriad of impossible to-dos. How will they purchase the prescription or bandages? How will they clean the wound without running water? How will they find their way back to the bridge they live under while injured? How can they elevate an injury while sleeping under a bush?

In this way, simple injuries progress into an unaddressed, ongoing disability. We have had several homeless cancer patients at tent city, a blind man, a deaf man and many who could not walk easily. Even with disability income from Social Security, they often did not have enough money for housing.

Mental Disability: Depression, Schizophrenia, Social and Generalized Anxiety, Anger Issues, Bipolar disorder, Obsessive Compulsive Disorder, and many other issues stand in the way of a homeless person even seeking treatment for their actual mental health issues, let alone seeking employment.

This camera-shy woman is heat drying screen-printed t-shirts she made in our Day Center's maker space.

Substance Abuse: The cycle of substance abuse is crippling and rehab facilities are expensive, often unavailable to felons, and have long waiting lists for anyone who cannot private pay. Even those who want help getting sober often cannot afford or find that help. Some succeed by their only available option, going cold turkey, only to become employed, have money and try drugs or alcohol "just one last time" to find themselves right back where they started.

Lack of Documentation: Life on the streets means life without safe storage. IDs, birth certificates, social security cards, health cards, food stamps and bus passes are stolen regularly. Having no transportation, no permanent address or no cash means reclaiming these lost items becomes near impossible without assistance. And it is nearly impossible to find gainful employment without these documents.

Criminal Records: Only around 40% of employers will even entertain the idea of hiring job applicants with a criminal record.[12] Having a criminal record and being visibly homeless can make gaining permanent work nearly impossible.

Now consider that statistic again -- 40% of homeless people work, even with one or many of the above common barriers in their way.

George attends church weekly and sings in the choir. He is very proud of his choir participation plaque.

Gary surveying our new house for the homeless. He is in charge of rehabbing the house.

Gary

Gary loves to work. He never stops moving. Gary was one of the lucky ones who found work even though he has a criminal record. But Gary also has a congenital heart condition that flares up in episodes that send him to a doctor for observation and medication. He became homeless after one of these episodes meant missing contract labor work.

"There are a lot of stereotypes out there," says Gary. "But anyone is one or two paychecks away from the curb. It's not always what you know, but who you know. If you don't have that support group then you don't have a backbone."

Gary's family lives in Florida and, while he loves them, he says they could not always be the support system he needed, as they were busy with their own needs and issues.

"I come from a family of outlaws. Dad, brother, aunts and uncles

This is Gary with his son, Gary Jr. They are working on the compost bin where we compost food scraps.

have all been to prison. I left home at 16. I had a step Dad that was there for me, but most everyone else wasn't available -- not to me, not to each other or society or anyone. When you don't have support as a child, what are you supposed to do? You start relying on yourself, just taking care of yourself and thinking no one wants you around. That's how I viewed the world. The world didn't want me. I think silver spoon types take their support networks for granted."

Gary says he made some mistakes in Florida and went to jail like the other men in his family. Then he got sober and decided to come to Ohio for a fresh start. But fresh starts are difficult with a criminal record.

"My felony was 20 years ago and they still pull it up. Society doesn't forgive felons. People look at a felon and think, 'I never did this. You must be a piece of trash.' I can't ever really get back into society."

But Gary had no trouble fitting in at the tent village. He says the folks at tent village became a family to him. He stayed in the village

These villagers are loading our truck to take trash up to our dumpster up the street. All villagers have to contribute an hour a day to the village.

for four months before finding new work and a place to live off the street, but he still volunteers with The Homeless Charity every day.

"I have been here in Akron a year and this tent city is my new family. I found my support system here. People at the bottom tend to be crabs in a bucket. They're pulling each other down and don't want to see other people succeed. But here in tent village, we're helping push each other out of the bucket. We're working against the stereotypes."

Everyone who lives in tent village is required to volunteer at least an hour a day to give back to the community and an hour a day working to improve their personal situation. When Gary came to the village he started volunteering at the facility 8-10 hours a day mostly in construction work. Gary built a wall in the day center, made a kitchen window pass through for a new section of the day center, created a mosaic wall of found objects, installed lights and now rehabs houses owned by The Homeless Charity.

Gary says, "I like to see where I can fit in and how I can help out. I

This is Gary painting our first house we purchased.

wanted to help get everything constructed properly at the day center. If we have better facilities up and running, then that helps the people here get themselves back up and running."

But it's about more than just giving back through manual labor for Gary. He feels like he can be a positive influence in the world again. He has found his value and worth.

"When you rub elbows with someone, you make an impact of some sort. So you should try and make a positive impact. People think they can't learn something from an addict or former prisoner or homeless person, but we might surprise you. I, myself, know how to work with my hands. I have an interesting perspective to share."

Gary is also sharing his construction work gifts with the homeless through his newly formed charity, Houses for The Homeless. Gary and his board of directors are raising funds to buy low income housing that the homeless will help rehab and then inhabit.

"Just yesterday I talked to a newspaper reporter. And he spoke to me because what we're doing here, and at my new charity, is important and positive. We're making a difference. We're giving back. We're doing what society should be doing and we matter."

Connecting People Who Need Houses With Houses That Need People.

Gary Mikes
Executive Director
(234) 206 - 0381

15 Broad St. Akron, OH 44305

garymikes@hfthomeless.com

...ses for the Homeless

This is Gary at his booth for the charity he started. He is a true success story of our village.

This is the first house we purchased. It is next door to our tent village.

Why Don't We Put These People in Abandoned Warehouses?

...or all these abandoned boarded up houses, or abandoned schools, or any structure that is being otherwise neglected?

Homeless are known to take care of themselves by doing just this very thing, although illegally. And many in society turn a blind eye as long as the person squatting is unseen and unheard.

When we bought our building at 15 Broad St., it had been empty for about 6 months and we found a mattress and a pair of old boots in the back corner of our basement. It was clear someone had made a home and we still scratch our heads wondering how the person was able to find entry.

Using abandoned shelter to house abandoned humans is the pinnacle of common sense. But, unfortunately, common sense is hard to come by in bureaucracy. Property owners, and the municipal-

This is Dave Murray putting up a tiny home he designed and built. So far, the city won't let him put these up anywhere legally.

ities that often take abandoned structures from those property owners, are bound by codes and laws.

The organizations that make those laws, and therefore stand in the way of simple solutions, don't mean to be ineffectively rigid, but they often are. And the humans working within these soul-less-seeming institutions feel there is little they can do fight the machine.

For example, no city will allow humans to inhabit a building that is not up to code. Period. Why? Because if they allow it then they are liable for anything that happens to any human in that structure. An improper installation of a fire door or a dead battery in an exit sign is enough to incriminate a property owner (including a city) for killing its occupants through neglect if there is a fire.

Abandoned structures don't always carry liability insurance (or any insurance at all), which leaves the owners susceptible to lawsuit if they were to haphazardly agree to allow someone inside. What if the person tripped and broke their hip or was startled and shot an intruder? It's a litigious world here in America. For better or worse, we often accomplish things through our court systems.

In the case of tent village at 15 Broad St., where the owners of the personal property are aware, give permission, have insurance, and follow every code recommendation, the city still will not permit the homeless camp because of zoning laws. Considering that, it's easy to see why empty structures remain empty.

A property owner, or even a municipality, may turn a blind eye to folks living in an abandoned structure or area, but they will never publicly approve or encourage it. They would argue that their hands are tied by the laws.

Akron Beacon Journal

OHIO.COM

Wednesday, October 17, 2018   Informing. Engaging. Essential. | 🐦 @ohiodotcom | f facebook.com/AkronBeaconJournal | $2

New Cavs era begins

To prove analysts and league insiders wrong, Cleveland players must overachieve

Maria Ridenour

INDEPENDENCE —
For the Cavaliers to buck daunting post-LeBron James odds this season, so much has to go right.

Kevin Love must avoid a major injury, which the five-time All-Star forward has been unable to do the past two seasons.

The Cavs must pick up the pace and at the same time avoid turning the ball over and firing up misguided missiles from beyond the arc.

Jordan Clarkson, Rodney Hood and Larry Nance Jr., acquired in February trades, and Cedi Osman must take a step forward.

Their defense, a regular-season afterthought during the previous four years with James, must become a nightly priority.

There's more. But in reality, the Cavs' challenge is easy to summarize. To prove analysts and league insiders wrong, they must overachieve.

History does not favor that happening, even as owner Dan Gilbert resisted the temptation to tank and signed Love to a four-year, $120 million contract extension three weeks after James bolted to the Los Angeles Lakers.

Gilbert's Cavs went 19-63

Group fights eviction of tent residents

Sage Lewis of the Homeless Charity on Tuesday talks about the Institute for Justice taking legal action against the city of Akron. (JEFF LANGE/AKRON.COM.CORRESPONDENT)

> This is a press conference where we announce we are going to appeal the city's decision to shut down our tent village.

By Doug Livingston
Beacon Journal/Ohio.com

National attorneys are suing the city of Akron for telling a private property owner that he must stop sheltering homeless people

tional ruling, he needs to continue the homeless-run campground. The operation, now 22 months running, had 43 residents then. The city and its homeless service partners in the Continuum of Care set a 60-day dead-

forward and help find the final people housing in the coming months," Heckman wrote in the email. "This is a community effort and without landlords or others willing to open their doors,

This is Paul finishing up a concrete floor he poured, sanded and sealed nearly single-handedly.

PAUL B

If you ask Paul if he's been homeless, he'll tell you he was only houseless.

"A home is just a place one abides to escape natural elements. I've built houses from the ground up. It was a gift passed off from my father. I excelled in building trades, so I never consider myself homeless. I can take cardboard and abide for a few hours. So, I've been houseless, but never homeless."

Before he was ever houseless, Paul lived a long and interesting life traveling overseas. He left Kent State University after the shootings and traveled abroad, spending over 25 years in third world countries working in infrastructure maintenance. He had considered dual citizenship with a West African nation, but ended up getting caught up in two different civil wars and eventually returned to the United States.

This is Paul digging through concrete to fix a clogged drain pipe.

Paul says living in war torn countries gave him a unique perspective on a lot of things, but homelessness especially. It seems to Paul that homeless people are often just refugees caught in their own personal wars.

He says, "This tent community is a refugee situation. We're not running from the bomb or bullet, but we tend to hide from, or look for safety from, the misunderstanding of the larger society. These people here have a lot of behavior issues and idiosyncrasies from past lifestyle circumstances and patterns. I think people here want to rebuild and reestablish themselves, but so much has taken place that sometimes they can't manage to reset and redirect, so they look for organizations like this one to help."

Paul found himself in need after the house where he was renting a room burned down. The fire started the day before Thanksgiving and Paul, with his maintenance experience, had even warned the owners that they needed to invest in a new thermostat, but Paul says they spent their money on a Thanksgiving feast instead and lost the whole house.

Paul is highly thoughtful and has a great deal of worldly experience.

"I had to jump out the window, roll off the roof and get to the next house's porch. I watched it burn to the ground. After that, I went to the local shelter for a week and then I came this direction and found tent city."

Once Paul got back on his feet, he decided to stay at the village because he liked the community and wanted to help make it a better place by becoming the on-site head of maintenance. He wanted to help transform the day center into a place for learning trade skills. Skill building, accountability and work ethic are all things Paul sees as being vital for the homeless looking to better themselves.

"If they have the will and impetus they can get out of being homeless, but sometimes people don't have an ideology and they get satisfied with being listless. Sometimes they get hopeless and give up. Or they feel persecuted. They need to see that no one will persecute you if you're being productive and helpful. But you can't just sit around and say 'I am homeless and I can't do nothing about it.' You've got to take your problems and do well by them. Make your

45 people make a lot of waste. But, if they did not live here, their trash might be on our streets.

worst assets your best assets."

Ultimately, Paul believes that community is key in the tent village and out in the wider world. He sees one problem shared by the homeless and the housed -- the false way we define our value. He believes that we cannot let industry and government define our worth.

"I believe when we consider the relevance and value of each other, we can learn the relevance and value of ourselves. We cannot allow the lesser part of our humanity and character to prevail over the greater part. The greatest gift you can give is actually the greatest gift to you. You give and you receive three fold."

Paul says he's been blessed and credits his own self reliance to his family and God.

"My father was my number one role model and God was his role model. I came from a nice lineage of people who had serenity."

But he also believes that serenity is available to all who want it: "We are all children of God. Our feet are all held by one gravity to one earth. We drink one water and breathe one air. Our skin, our accent, our nationality is a minor difference to the major, which is that we are all equal in the eyes of God."

This is Willy and Sully after a full day of work at the village.

This is Ethan. He's never touched drugs and only drank alcohol a couple times in his life.

Aren't All Homeless People Addicts?

Not all, but many. Agencies find it difficult to count, but estimate around 60-70% of homeless people are addicted to drugs or alcohol.

According to Substance Abuse and Mental Health Services Administration estimates, 38% of homeless people were dependent on alcohol and 26% abused other drugs.[13] As one might expect, the relationship between drugs and homelessness can be complicated.

Addiction disrupts relationships, support systems, employment, and, for those already struggling to pay bills, it can lead to homelessness. A survey by the United States Conference of Mayors asked 25 cities for their top three causes of homelessness. Substance abuse was the single largest cause of homelessness for single adults. However, for some, substance abuse is the result of being homeless. Drug use also gives temporary relief to people coping with the difficult situation of homelessness.[14]

This is Brian. He stayed with us for some time. Then he moved back to the woods and we lost contact with him.

For many homeless people, mental illness is the bigger problem and substance abuse is a way to self medicate unsuccessfully. Being addicted and mentally ill is a hallmark curse in the homeless community and being without stable shelter makes recovery from both issues a huge obstacle, especially when the hazard of life on the streets is added into the mix -- risks like violent victimization, ER visits, jail visits and limited access to recovery facilities. [15]

This is a quagmire to put it mildly. Breaking addiction is difficult. Poverty and homelessness adds another layer of complication to something already extremely complicated. The current accepted solution is "housing first;" the idea being that once homelessness is eliminated, obstacles to addiction recovery fall away.

But considering that much of the homeless population became homeless because of addiction issues, why would placing them back in a home actually help that situation? That was, after all, how they began their journey to the streets. Then again, leaving them on the streets becomes a societal and humanitarian crisis.

At tent village, we find what helps many of our recovering addicts is the stability of shelter with a community of support. Our members become a part of our community by agreeing to a written understanding that they will "move their lives forward" in the area of addiction, homelessness and joblessness.

The accountability for this creed is the mandatory reporting of at least one hour of time, per day, spent toward this pursuit. Attending a recovery class, making a phone call, applying for employment, seeing a therapist, all counts toward the goal of "moving your life forward." They also are required to spend another hour in their day helping others in the community through volunteering.

Members of tent village, who follow the agreement, experience an average stay of 4-6 months before finding permanent housing. Housing first, while providing stable sheltering, does not offer bundled support beyond a place to exist safely. We are communal, social creatures that need community for our wellbeing. It is our opinion that taking this fact into account is essential, not only in helping the homeless, but for helping those suffering from addiction as well.

This Councilwoman Tara Samples with Sage. She has supported us fully since the beginning.

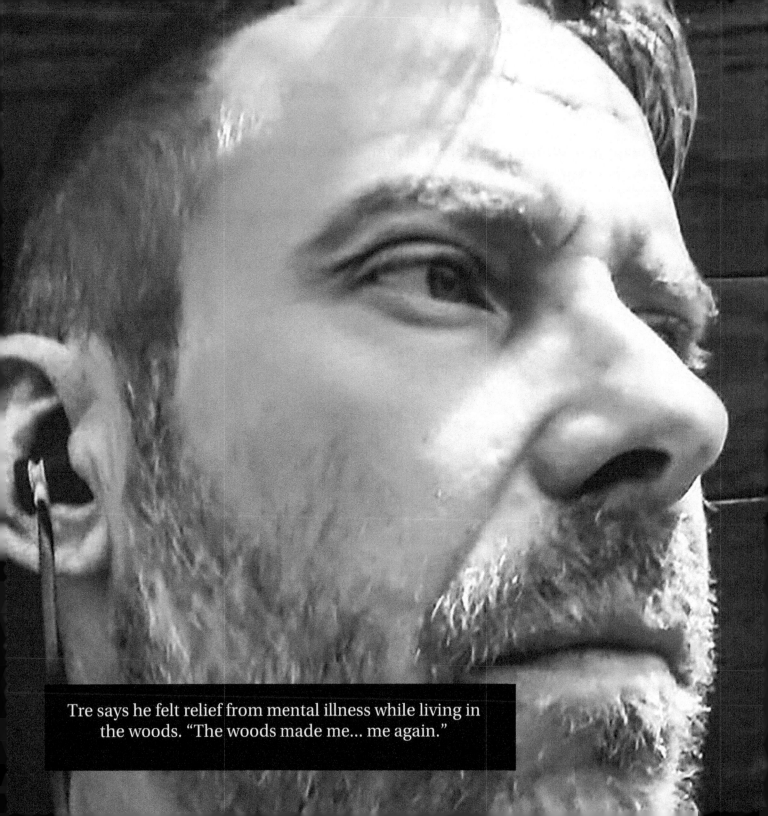

Tre says he felt relief from mental illness while living in the woods. "The woods made me... me again."

Tre

Tre Shotwell was a construction manager for a roofing company and had several teams he supervised. He made $60,000, he and his wife lived in a large home in Akron, and he drove a new truck. When he got laid off, he fell behind on his truck payments. While the vehicle was being repoed, Tre helped the tow truck driver load it up and the repo man liked him so much he offered him a job.

At first it was ideal. The bills were paid and he loved the work. They called him, "The Bulldog."

Tre says, "I would tell people, 'I'm just here doing my job.' I liked it. It was different and I was kind of getting paid to steal stuff legally. It was crazy pulling stuff out of folks driveway while they're sleeping. You don't even need the keys."

But, on one job, Tre and his partner ran into trouble and both of them were beaten severely. Tre never went back to work and found

Alice and Brian in front of their American flag in front of their tent.

himself suffering from near insurmountable mental health issues.

"My partner was almost beat to death. They stole the tow truck. That incident changed my life. I tried to keep working, but I didn't trust anyone. I thought everyone was out to get me. I lost touch with reality for a bit. I became antisocial, depressed, stayed in my room all day. Then I started thinking my wife was trying to kill me and I started using some drugs. Things fell apart. Eventually, we lost our home."

Tre and his wife spent the last of their savings staying at a Red Roof Inn, but ,when the money was gone, they were standing in the parking lot with their last belongings and nowhere to go.

"We were standing with our bags, under a tree. I saw a path into the woods and I said, 'Let's go.' My wife started screaming and yelling and crying and calling me every name in the book and I said, 'I know. I know, but if you want to survive this, just follow me.'"

Tre made a lean to out of sticks and trash in an encampment other

This is Amani Abraham from WKYC TV. She is doing a live feed from our village here. She regularly reports on our village.

homeless had abandoned. He got himself and his wife out of the rain that night. It was the beginning of their homelessness.

Eventually, the couple made other homeless friends, formed a makeshift camp, and started dumpster diving to sell found objects for income. They were given an old tent by another homeless person and used the money they made to buy a small cook stove and some utensils.

Tre says, "We made it work."

But things went from bad to worse when Tre was picked up on a warrant. He and his wife had heard about the tent village, but didn't think they needed additional help.

"As they were putting me in the cop car, I told her, 'Go over to tent village!' I was in jail for a week, and, when I came out, I came right over here. I literally ran from the jail.

When they told me my wife was here and she was safe, we both em-

These villagers are clearing our second lot where we expanded. It is next to our house we own.

braced and were crying. I was so worried she'd get hurt. I owe that to you guys. She was safe here."

Tre stayed at the tent village for about eight months and took on many opportunities and positions as he worked on his mental health issues.

"I liked being a staff member and being an essential part of making and establishing this place. It wasn't a power trip; it was about making a difference. It felt good to be a part of something. And I learned a lot about myself and so much about a lot of people."

One thing Tre learned was that his mental issues were actually easier to handle out in the woods and at tent village. He felt like spending time, in nature, without material possessions, helped him heal.

He says, "Going into the woods made me… me again. There was a peacefulness of being alone. And it allowed me to get better and socialize more. I was at peace as a homeless person, but my wife hated it. Being homeless helped me regain who I was, but, unfortunately, I lost my wife. She needed security and I couldn't give it to her. That broke me. That's the lowest point of my life. She is my best friend."

Tre has had a few jobs since he left tent village and, for now, he has a place in a house and job again. He has hope for the future, but also a few regrets.

"I hate that I lost myself and I lost my wife. But she'll always be there as a friend."

This is Aimee. She ran our administration work for quite some time.

Brett panhandles mostly for food because he uses his food card to buy food for his kids.

Aren't Panhandlers just Scam Artists?

There have been many local and national exposes on professional panhandlers. Some make $100,000 in a year, get into nice cars after their eight hours on a sidewalk corner, and form networks worthy of scam investigations.[16] "Donors Beware" is fair warning when giving to those begging at intersections.

And where does the money go once it's into the person's hands? Most charitable organizations that work with the homeless sensibly take the position that money is better spent through non profit networks that serve the needy directly. Put the money into professional hands. Don't give money to a drug habit.

But, we at The Homeless Charity know of people who panhandle to help pay medical bills or buy things food cards don't cover like adult diapers for their incontinence. That's why The Homeless Charity stays neutral on the issue because we personally know

This is from our 2018 Friendsgiving. Villagers and supporters come together to eat and listen to music.

many panhandlers, and their stories greatly vary.

We also know that many charitable organizations are not permitted legally, or by their nonprofit rules and regulations, to give money to someone desperately in need of cash -- even if it is for a cancer prescription, feminine hygiene products, or to make up a deficit for one month's room rent. Even if they know that person is hard working and it's a one-time request, they are bound by their own bureaucratic rules to not help.

It's difficult to formerly come out against panhandling when you know people who may genuinely need a hand up in a desperate moment. For example, we know several panhandlers with criminal records who cannot find steady W-2 employment because of their felonies, but hustle for seasonal work. They only "fly a sign" when the landscaping and roofing and construction work dries up. They do it to make their room rent in the cold months.

So what's to be done about the "Panhandler Problem?"

And it is a problem. It's a problem for a few reasons. Economically struggling cities, like Akron, Ohio, with its debt approaching 1 billion, are trying desperately to convince people to move into their neighborhoods and support their infrastructure.[17] Cities realize that panhandlers on every corner detract from accomplishing this mission. One can easily argue that panhandlers and vagrants stand in the way of helping stimulate normal economic development and health for towns and cities.

So, why not make it illegal? Many try and that's a problem too. Several court cases have ruled that municipalities that make non-confrontational panhandling illegal are violating people's first amendment rights.[18]

And then there's the issue of humanitarianism, the moral issue, which falls to all of us. Do we simply not want to see the unfortunate results of income inequality? While we may feel better believing all panhandlers are scam artists or drug addicts, that is simply not always the case.

These are supporters surrounded by villagers. Having volunteers and villagers work together is an important part of our mission.

This is John panhandling for a little extra money. He also gets disability payments, but they do not always cover expenses, which include student loans.

John

John is what most in the homeless service community would call a success story. John is a disabled felon who found himself on the street after his release from prison. He had never been homeless before he went to jail.

"I got out in November and had nowhere to go. I got a beer that night, just one, and walked over to the shelter. I had to blow a breathalyser to get in and got banned. I didn't know that would happen. Someone in line told me they'd take me at the drop in center for addicts and drunks, but when I went there I wasn't drunk enough to get in. That night, I actually panhandled, for beer money, so I could get drunk enough to have a place to sleep. That was the night I learned you either have to be completely sober or a drunk to get off the street."

After figuring that out, John learned from others about tent city,

Ashleigh, seen here talking with a villager, is a high school student that volunteers with us each week.

a place that took you as is, but required sobriety moving forward. John says he was never "a drunk." He just needed a second chance.

"I lived here for two months. Got my disability benefits in order, saved money and got a place. Next, I want to go back to school, but I have to pay my student loans back from when I went the first time. So, basically, I need to get a job."

This is proving problematic because of his disability and his criminal record. John wants to put his past behind him, but feels like other people are not always willing to do the same.

"Sometimes it feels like other people get in my way. You feel like you're spinning your wheels and you start losing hope. I found a job with help from a service, but I lost it because of my disability issues. They are helping me look for new work now."

While looking for work, John still occasionally panhandles to make ends meet. He has not yet qualified for a food card because of transportation issues. He knows he needs to get to the required, in-person appointments to qualify, but until he gets this done, covering expenses can get down to the wire.

"I live in a house, renting a room with 4 other people. I've been there for four months. I get $740 from the government each month. $375 goes to rent, $70 goes to my phone, I pay the student loan minimum and the rest goes to food. I usually come up a little short and that's when I panhandle."

John laughed when told about scam artists that makes thousands of dollars a year: "If I get a good corner, I can make $15 in about 4 or so hours. I went out today though and only got a $1 and a sandwich. It was a good sandwich. But I did better the day I flew the sign that said, 'I need beer money.'"

This is councilman Zack Milkovich on the left. He took some villagers to Stark State College in Akron to learn about programs they could take to help with job training.

This is Vincent, the raccoon, in our moldy bread box before it got to the compost bin.

Why Are the Mentally Ill on The Streets?

According to HUD's 2016 Annual Homelessness Assessment Report, one in five homeless people experience a serious mental illness, meaning their mental state negatively affects their ability to function in society.[19] Why are they wandering our streets?

Treatment options, for most, are limited. Some argue they are limited to an emergency room or jail. Psychiatric beds and long term care facilities for the mentally ill, fell out of favor beginning in the 1960s and the trend continues to this day, resulting in a severe shortage of "psych ward" beds in hospitals.

There are virtually no more long term, residential facilities for the mentally ill in operation. The exception are a very few facilities accepting private pay. These facilities are not available to working class and low income mentally ill people. They cannot gain access to that level of care through insurance.

This was our village in May of 2017. We had about 6 tents and were just beginning our formal charity.

The trend to shut down institutions was well intentioned. It began with the Community Mental Health Act in 1963 when institutionalized patients were released to more mainstream accommodations, like group homes or rooms for rent, with community based care as the new course of action.[20]

But those community care options didn't materialize in great enough number to match more severe mental health needs. The result was that those who needed help the most began losing their housing. Now there is a nationwide lack of beds for the mentally ill. And those homeless people with serious mental health issues now flood emergency rooms and are simply turned back onto the street.[21] There is nowhere for them to go.

Which leads to a different kind of institutionalization for the seriously mentally ill. Homeless mentally ill are more likely to be incarcerated than their non-mentally ill homeless counterparts. And one study suggests that those who would have been formerly placed in mental institutions are now simply placed in jail.[22]

We have seen this ourselves many times. We know a schizophrenic man who is able to work, be social and contribute to society, but when he misses a few pills and has an episode, he falls back into errant behavior, loses his work, and returns to the street. A different homeless man in our village suffered so acutely from PTSD after a violent attack, that he became non verbal and unable to care for himself. We took him to the local ER hoping someone could help. He was evaluated and released within one day and wandered back to our facility dazed, still mute and barefoot.

Unfortunately, there are endless examples of severely mentally ill men and women on our streets whose illness has taken them out of society. We can do better. Many believe adding psychiatric beds is essential in helping people escape the condition of homelessness.

Our first computer lab had 3 computers. We have 12 computers now on site for homeless use.

This is Robin with his girlfriend Joyce.

Robin

Robin lived in Bath, Ohio with his wife of 21 years. They owned a nice home, two cars and had assets. He ran two pet stores and she worked for the Department of Defense for 25 years.

"Those were the best years of my life," says Robin. "People think the homeless are all on drugs. It's not just people doing heroin and meth. People are out here grieving and having mental health issues."

For Robin, it was severe grief and depression after a traumatic event that sent him into the streets.

"My story started 10 years ago. My wife was diagnosed with MS. The last five years of her life, she was in a coma from a midline shift -- a brain and spinal cord aneurysm that pushed her brain three millimeters over. She went to work one day, gave me a kiss, an hour later her boss called and said she was being taken to City Hospital.

Our raised bed gardens were built during the first summer of the village's inception.

It was a just a normal day. The last thing I heard from her was 'I love you. I'll see you tonight.'"

She never spoke again and remained in a coma for the next five years. Robin and his sister cared for her at home and Robin never gave up hope that one day his wife might wake up and be okay again.

Robin said, "I kept hope alive, because of my faith. I thought there was a chance, even though doctors told me there wasn't."

Then there was an electrical fire in their home. It started from a short in an extension cord Robin had plugged in around the Holidays. He was able to get to his wife out of the house, but he didn't realize that the smoke she inhaled had damaged her delicate lungs. She died three days later.

"I lost my wife and my house and my life in an instant."

Robin blamed himself for his wife's death and fell into a deep de-

This is our village in June of 2017. We had about 12 tents at this time. Around this time, our residents organized their security team and tri-council.

pression. His homeowners insurance had lapsed and he turned away everyone's help. He didn't take anything from his sister, his extended family, friends, or even the Red Cross.

"After the funeral, I disappeared. I grabbed some tarps I had on my property and I left. I became homeless because I thought I deserved it. It was my fault. I'd killed her. I ended up making a tent over on what they call 'Tweaker Hill.' I didn't feel I deserved my family. I wouldn't go to counseling. I didn't want to feel better. I wouldn't leave my tent or eat and I lost 140 pounds."

After almost two years on Tweaker Hill someone encouraged Robin to come and get clothes and food at The Homeless Charity Day Center.

"I still only had my clothes that were damaged in the fire. I could smell the smoke, every day. I came and got nice new clothes. I was proud to wear them."

Robin started coming to the center once a week and then went

Twice a week, the charity and villagers hold meetings to discuss issues.

back to his tent. But, each time he came, he talked to more and more people. People that had made mistakes and were trying to get better, just like him.

"After talking to people here, I realized other people had circumstances like mine. They made mistakes and became homeless too. Then the city gave me seven days to move off Tweaker Hill. So I came over here and you told me to come on in. You guys saw something in me. And you let me in here and everyone here turned my life around."

It was around that same time that Robin learned he had terminal cancer. "Turns out I have small cell cancer and it went through my lungs and started into my spinal cord. At first, I figured it's God's revenge and I refused to take my cancer medicine."

But soon his friends at the tent village, who Robin calls family, helped him change his mind.

"I opened up here. I started sharing my views. The people here take you in and look out for you. My life has meaning again and it's all because of this charity. God had a purpose for me. He didn't give me a hill I couldn't climb. I am here to help people. I give back now and it makes me feel better."

Robin stayed at tent village for two months and began collecting SSI and got an apartment right down the street from the village. He's proud that he's collecting money he and his wife earned during their years of work and that he got an apartment without government assistance.

He still has bad dreams about the fire that keep him awake, so he volunteers as a security guard at night. He still won't see a counselor, but says that with the little time he has left, he just wants to live his life and help people while he can. He takes his cancer medication now.

"I love life now. I have purpose. This place gave me purpose and no one knew it. Closing this down will be devastating. Other people need this place."

Before our compost bin, we took our food waste to Frankie the pig.

From left this is: Steve, Jon and Ronnie. They revived a villager who had an overdose. He would have died without them.

How Can We Better Help Homeless People?

Beggars. Vagabonds. Gypsies. Hobos. We have lived with the homeless, arguably, since human society began. We ask the question, over and over, why does this happen? Why is it that some people cannot be part of the larger society? And what do we do, if anything, to help these people stay safe and survive?

We feel that helping the homeless requires more than just a willingness a help. It requires acknowledging and addressing some key issues.

First and foremost, we must begin to see homelessness as a complex condition. A person becomes homeless for a myriad of reasons, which when combined, create a tangle of individualized and nuanced barriers to societal reintegration. We tend to want to compartmentalize homeless people because it makes things easier -- addicts, mentally ill, lazy -- but we have to realize labels stand in the way of comprehensive solutions.

This is Cloud enjoying a pastry donated from Panera.

Homeless people are not just drug addicted, mentally ill, or behaviorally deviant, which means addiction recovery centers, hospitals and therapists cannot individually solve this issue. They must work together. And while most homeless people have extremely low income, HUD and housing first initiatives cannot solve the problem alone either, because of the individualized issues like those mentioned above.

In the business world, experts speak of how "siloed" departments can run a company amuck. When specialists do not work together, projects fail. Homelessness, as a social improvement project, is arguably failing. In our opinion, the failure exists at the nonprofit and government bureaucratic level. Those in positions of power are often unwilling to address homelessness as a multifaceted condition that requires innovative and individualized solutions.

For example, placing a person, with extreme social anxiety, in a room for rent with shared space, is not going to keep that person off the street even if the room is paid for entirely. That individual

Sometimes, we have our mandatory meetings outdoors in the village.

will not be able to function in that environment and will flee back to the street.

Similarly, a behaviorally deviant person might be willing to be housed in a group environment, but unable to follow the rules required and also be kicked out. All said to illustrate that well-meaning and generous housing first initiatives can easily fail and put certain homeless back on the street in a very brief time period.

We once put a chronically homeless woman in a room in a shared house and she immediately had problems. She started storing her items on the roof that extended below her window. She wouldn't use the clothes dryer, but instead hung her clothes to dry outside where it was not permitted. She would leave her room regularly to sleep by the railroad tracks in the grass with her dog. Eventually, living in the house was too much. She left and went back to her tent in the woods. She had been homeless for over a decade and simply couldn't conform to living inside again.

Another woman who has lived in the woods since she was 13, due

A villager found this license plate and put it on the back of his cart he uses for dumpster diving.

to severe anxiety, collects no social services and never goes to a doctor or a mental health professional. She did, however, start using our shower and laundry facility at The Homeless Charity Day Center. Just when we were making progress in getting her further mental health assistance, the city found her extremely hidden camp and made her move. Now she's disappeared.

These examples illustrate why affordable housing is not really the singular issue facing municipalities with homeless people. And yet, "no affordable housing," along with its solution-based counterpart, "housing first" have become the labels and compartments that oversimplify the homeless condition. It is our opinion that housing first ideals often stand in the way of solving homelessness.

As an example, in our town of Akron, Ohio, there are affordable rooms for rent. There are also, in theory, rooms available through government programs if one sits on a waiting list. And there are usually a few beds available for a limited time in emergency shelters.

This is Akron's Fire Chief Clarence Tucker. The fire department came to inspect regularly.

This allows a city like ours to say things like, "We do not have a homeless problem," when there are still clearly many individuals sleeping on park benches and in doorways.

What they mean to say is, "we *should not* have a homeless problem." They have all the proper channels in place to house homeless individuals, so those on the street must "want" to be there. "Want," of course, is not the right word. They are unable to conform to requirements -- either to qualify for housing or to stay in it. That does not mean they are choosing or wanting to be homeless.

Yet few feel empowered to address why the existing channels are not working. This blindspot, this collective shrug, can lead to bureaucratic absurdity. One where a government official will say "there is no homeless problem in our town," while driving past dozens of homeless people on their way to work.

There are, in fact, some homeless people that even nonprofits who work with the population will acknowledge are "unhouseable." People with felonies and no income are particularly likely to fall

These are high school student volunteers who helped clean out part of our building to make more space.

into this category. Yet, one could argue, these are exactly those we do not want to step around on our downtown sidewalks.

Others are houseable on paper, but due to various factors, they cannot manage the bureaucratic system as required to obtain housing. Housing, even being placed on a housing wait list, requires a homeless person to travel to multiple appointments and pay fees to obtain proper identification, receive said identification in the mail, fill out applications with agencies, and answer and make phone calls to follow up on in-person appointments.

Someone with a mental or physical disability, a mental illness, or even zero income would struggle to meet these requirements even if they could try and meet them from a warm and safe place. Yet they are asked to do it while surviving the harsh conditions of living on the street. Is it any wonder many find it impossible?

And where do those on the wait list stay -- those who fulfill all requirements and yet cannot be housed for over six months to three years? If the local shelters have stay limits or their own wait lists, as

SPORTS, G1

Browns fall

Kizer at QB

CLEVELAND 8

THIS PLACE, THIS TIME, B1

Infamous doctor sought refuge in wrestling ring

ease from prison

Y, B1

esidents exceed expectations in signing up to hash out solutions

> The Akron Beacon Journal has covered our entire journey. We have been front page news many times.

Akron's homeless

PITCHING IN TO SURVIVE

ond Chance Village tent city focuses on big picture: helping homeless to help themselves and take a leading role in bettering their lives

Around midday in July, it's musty cool in the basement of 15 Broad

Paul Hays, who manages The meless Charity, a not-for-prof navigates a maze of unfinished ms with odds and ends stacked st-high in piles spread across the crete floor.

Keeping up with donations from rches and the community is a ly chore. Some of the items come m Sage Lewis, the property own who passes along anything left r from his auctions to support homeless.

Hays, 52, advanced a thrift store donation center to sell salvage e items. The Second Chance Store, as it's called, is just the first step to ward establishing fi nancial sustainability at the Second Chance Village in the Middle bury neighborhood, Akron's new home for

Stories
by
Doug
ngston

Photos

they do in Akron, Ohio (and many other cities), then the homeless must survive on the streets. Often for years.

If we're going to make progress towards solving homelessness, we have to admit that what we're doing currently is not enough. We have to admit that shelters were created for emergencies and not for people on three year waiting lists for housing assistance. We have to admit that affordable housing is not the only barrier to housing the homeless. And, perhaps most importantly, we have to believe homelessness is an issue worth solving.

We have made progress in America understanding the complication of things like drug addiction, alcohol addiction... even sex addiction. We see them now as a complex net of cognitive and behavioral patterns that manifest themselves in self-limiting and unhealthy behaviors. And yet we tend to look at homelessness as a housing issue instead of a complex condition. We let ourselves believe that people in the street deserve and want to be there.

There is no one size fits all solution to fix homelessness and yet innovative solutions to addressing the issue, in new ways, are often rejected before given a proper chance to thrive. Those in leadership positions, in nonprofits and governments alike, don't want to admit failings or lose funding. This often puts innovative problem solving at risk.

These villagers are tearing up an old floor for what is now our fully remodeled community room.

A tiny house transitional village in Eugene Oregon. One innovative solution to the problem of homelessness.

The Innovators

We, as a nation, are stuck in this "housing first" mindset. Theoretically, it is the right mindset. A house gives the person shelter and a place to sleep. A house also solves some safety needs such as personal security. It's important to know that it is nearly impossible to deal with things like getting a job and recovering from addiction if you don't have these fundamental needs met.

But the problem we're experiencing is that housing first, in its current popular manifestation, begins with the creation of more affordable / low-income housing, which can save people from homelessness. Building affordable housing is vitally important, but it does little to help the currently and chronically homeless in America.

We must look at American homelessness for what it is: an economic and social disaster. These people need to get the same imme-

This is our villager Eric talking about addiction issues with another villager. Homeless helping homeless is at the core of our program.

diate treatment that tornado, volcano and earthquake survivors receive. We should ask ourselves, why are we so unwilling to see this as a humanitarian crisis?

Many homeless advocates are fearful of new ideas that seek to supplement the existing shelter and housing-first system. Even, Maria Foscarinis, the executive director of the National Law Center on Homelessness & Poverty, a nonprofit legal group in Washington, D.C. told the New York Times, "Seattle is doing some things that are fairly innovative. But the encampments are there because of the failure to create affordable, decent housing. I absolutely fear that they will be seen as the solution."[23]

If we don't test innovative solutions because we're afraid, if we don't address the immediate need because we cling to an ideal, then the homeless will continue to suffer. We cannot let elitism, idealism or a love of the status quo hurt the homeless that are on the street today. We have a moral obligation to embrace innovative solutions.

15
Broad St.

FEED PEOPLE.
FIGHT HUNGER.

FOOD
BANK

VEHICLE GENEROUSLY FUNDED BY Walmart

This is the Food Bank coming to support us. We run a
food pantry for the entire neighborhood.

Seattle is dealing with this crisis head on. They have seven sanctioned tiny home villages.[24] Others have created villages out of tents with the intention of building tiny homes in the future. Besides Seattle, there are a few notable sanctioned tent communities in America including, Hope Village in La Cruces, NM[25], Opportunity Village in Eugene, OR[26] and Community First Village in Austin, TX[27]. All have been either approved or supported by their local municipalities. All offer community support and individualized service to the homeless awaiting affordable housing.

Tent communities, almost universally, have come at the homeless condition from a revolutionary direction.

- They are mostly democratically lead by the residents themselves.
- They require a work contribution to build a collaborative community where people feel part of something important.
- They personalize the help they give residents to address their individual barrier to being housed.

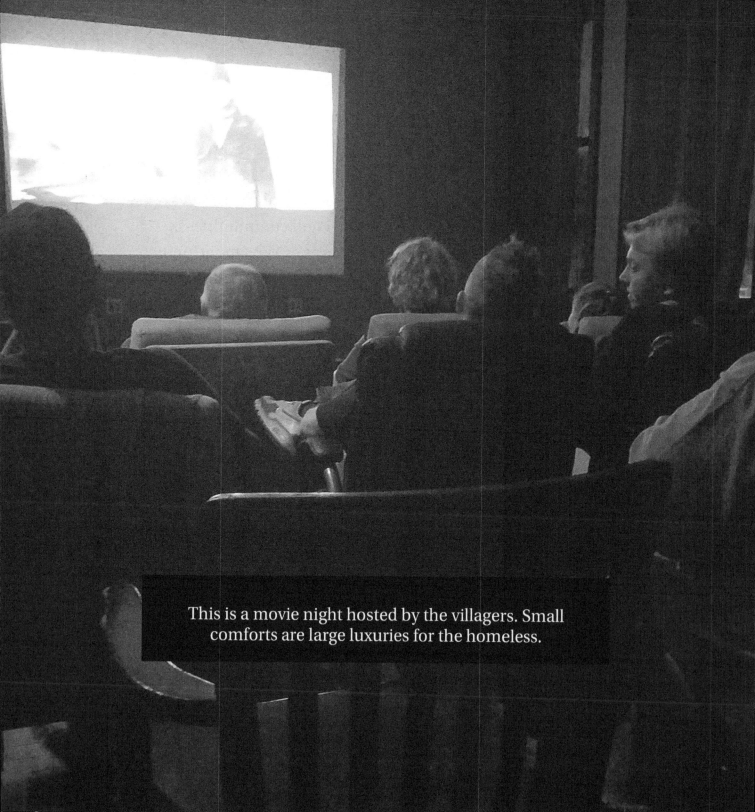

This is a movie night hosted by the villagers. Small comforts are large luxuries for the homeless.

While approved camps are rare, underground camps are everywhere and on the rise. In the last nine years there has been a 1,342 percent increase in known homeless camps.[28] And, to be fair, most camps are not known and hide themselves as well as possible, since when found they are quickly deemed illegal and residents are forced to move.

In fact, our tent village, which sheltered homeless during the latest U.S. Census Bureau point in time count, "made" the homeless population of Akron increase by 71%. The city, in fact, blamed our camp for increasing homelessness, when the more logical explanation is that we simply sheltered homeless from already existing, hidden encampments in the city.[29] Those hidden and never-before counted were suddenly counted.

Tents are not ideal human habitation, but they are better than nothing. And nothing is often and ironically the accepted option for those being "saved" from tent living through legal enforcement.

Tents are also an affordable way to serve the population effectively.

Our village at full capacity in the spring of 2018.

The cost to shelter and feed each resident, per day, at The Homeless Charity Village is $4.00 per person and costs taxpayers $0. HUD estimates that sheltering a homeless person in an emergency shelter is the least expensive option, and yet it costs, on average, $19 per day in Des Moines, IA, $44 a day in Houston, TX, $22 in Jackson, FL.[30]

Not only are tent villages a cheaper solution than traditional shelters, we argue they are better, because they offer the homeless what they want -- a safe and legal place to exist, day and night, and a place to securely store their things while they work to find housing.

Even if canvas is not ideal over drywall, wood and shingles, we must consider the alternative for many. In our town, there is NO alternative due to shelter wait lists and stay limits. This is the case in many cities.

Kathleen, a woman in her fifties, came to us in October after a recent eviction. She was in a state of total panic. She works 50 hours a week on an assembly line and was living in her car, but law en-

This is Kathleen. She came to us desperate because all women's shelters were full and the police threatened to arrest her if they caught her sleeping again in her car.

forcement kept finding her and eventually threatened her with jail if they found her sleeping in her car again.

She had been to every single shelter in town and the waiting list had her earliest date of service at three weeks. She was asked to return and check daily, but she could barely get there during their hours because of work. She knew, if she could not find a place to park her car or lay her head, she would lose her job and then really be in trouble.

We made space for Kathleen. How could we not? How could leave this poor, desperate, hard working woman under a bridge for three or more weeks knowing she would lose her job?

Why would it be legal for Kathleen to huddle under an overpass for three weeks, but not legal for her to stay in a nice new tent, in a safe community, near a warm, accessible structure with needed facilities? We cannot sacrifice good enough for a perfect ideal that is not coming to fruition.

These are supporters and villagers gathering for a tour. Many people's eyes were opened by a tour of our facility.

If the homeless will choose to camp in these safe facilities, but will not or can not find emergency brick and mortar shelter, we maintain that it is inhumane to close those facilities down. For the record, modern technology has made tents able to withstand temperatures as low as -60 degrees Fahrenheit.

Tents are also self contained, provide affordable privacy, and are easy to erect, take down, and clean up after. The other beauty of a tent is that it is transitional. Municipalities often speak of not "enabling" the homeless by making their temporary housing too appealing. We know of one homeless nonprofit director who says, unapologetically, that street life is "motivating" to people that need to make their way through the red tape of affordable housing assistance programs.

With no sense of irony, many will claim that tents are inhumane shelter options in one breath, and then in the next say those same tents enable homeless by making them too comfortable.

The party line seems to be: "We can't think putting people in tent villages is the solution. The only solution is more housing for the extremely poor." That's a fine mission, but it's not an either / or scenario. Let's be honest. There will not be, in the near future, enough housing to address the complicated and overwhelming problem of homelessness in 21st century America.

The reality is that we have to consider all our options until there are no more people lying in the streets and there are no more people acceptably labeled "un-housable." If there are no better options and the homeless choose tent villages, ask for tent villages, and are willing to move themselves from tent villages into affordable housing, then tent villages need to be an option.

The essence of innovation is to come at a problem more efficiently and effectively. Right now, tent villages do exactly that. What if we put tents in abandoned warehouses or heated pole barns? What if we put a tiny home on the back lot of every church in America?

If we do not ask these questions and consider new answers, we will not solve homelessness in America.

The New York Times

Why a Private Landowner Is Fighting to Keep the Homeless on His Property

Our village's fight with the City of Akron was covered by The New York Times. We represent an issue all of America faces.

This is Jim. He runs our clothing room. He is an incredibly proud, dignified man. He now has a home.

Moving Forward as a Nation

Innovations in homeless care and service will move us forward as a nation. A rising tide lifts all boats, and, when the least among us is served, it serves us all. But, do we believe it?

The campaign for hearts and minds, in any social justice movement, is key. Our nation's homeless need a public relations advocate. They have been labeled, stereotyped and demonized. Many believe they do not deserve help. Many take this position without apology: That they deserve life on the street. They are failures and they should live with the consequences of that failure.

It's our position that dehumanizing anyone hurts us all. You don't need to be a heart broken humanitarian to see that leaving our streets littered with "failed" humans who could not perform in society -- literally festering in their own filth and starving -- is not good for any community.

It's not good from a sanitation perspective alone. Many outbreaks

This is Willie (from the cover). He LOVES to color. After 50 years of being homeless, he now has a home.

of Hepatitis A have been linked to the unserviced homeless.[31] If not concerned about health, how about economics? A chronically homeless person costs the taxpayer an average of $35,578 per year. And then there is crime. Studies have shown that homeless individuals are more likely to be jailed for property crimes, such as theft, and nuisance crimes associated with being homeless, such as loitering, sleeping in a car or in public, or trespassing.[32]

We would argue that people who have nothing, have nothing to lose, and that makes them vulnerable, but also reckless. They have nothing, so why not take what they need… from you? And this is not just a danger to our "stuff," but a waste of our precious policing resources. Law enforcement should be focused on more important issues than petty theft and loitering.

So, even if a person is "heartless" towards the conditions faced by homeless, we would hope they can see the personal gain in helping those in need. For those who have a heart, or respect the teachings of religion, there should be a humanitarian calling to care for the homeless.

We all need to do a better job of seeing extremely low income people as humans with equal rights. Classism is real. No one wants to live next to a poor person and they really don't want to live next to a homeless person. Not one they can actually see, anyway.

We need to realize that homeless people have value. We do not need to just warehouse or hide them or wish them dead. Many homeless go on to do wonderful things with their lives and contribute greatly to society. Don't they all deserve a chance? Don't they all deserve to live?

Once we can acknowledge that the least among us are human, then we can acknowledge that stepping over humans living on the street, with nothing, is a humanitarian crisis.

Epilogue

As of print time, the City of Akron had ordered the tents removed from 15 Broad Street by the start of 2019. While we are continuing to battle this order through the court system, with the help of non profit lawyers from The Institute for Justice, we are also obeying the current law and removing the tents.

Sadly, many homeless remain on our streets on wait lists, unable to get into full shelters, and freezing cold under bridges and bushes. Yet, the city says, "The System Works."

It may be the end of our tents, but our community can never be dismantled. Our day center will remain open and expand, we will triple outreach efforts to those left outdoors, and we will keep purchasing houses to shelter those on wait lists and in transition.

Follow our story at TheHomelessCharity.org.

Bibliography

1. National Health Care for the Homeless Council, Addressing the Opioid Epidemic: How the Opioid Crisis Affects Homeless Populations Fwwact Sheet, https://www.nhchc.org/wp-content/uploads/2017/08/nhchc-opioid-fact-sheet-august-2017.pdf (August 2017).

2. Edward O. Wilson, *as quoted in The Social Conquest of Earth,* Natalie Angier, *in Smithsonian Magazine,* "Edward O. Wilson's New Take on Human Nature," *https://www.smithsonianmag.com/science-nature/edward-o-wilsons-new-take-on-human-nature-160810520/ (April 2012)*

3. Phillip Connor and Jens Manuel Krogstad, For the first time, U.S. resettles fewer refugees than the rest of the world, http://www.pewresearch.org/fact-tank/2018/07/05/for-the-first-time-u-s-resettles-fewer-refugees-than-the-rest-of-the-world/ (July 5, 2018)

4. U.S. Department of Health and Human Services, Administration for Children and Families, Administration on Children, Youth and Families, Children's Bureau, Trends in Foster Care and Adoption, https://www.acf.hhs.gov/cb/resource/trends-in-foster-care-and-adoption (October 20, 2017)

5. U.S. Department of Health and Human Services, Administration for Children and Families, Administration on Children, Youth and Families, Children's Bureau. Child Maltreatment 2016: Reports from the States to the National Child Abuse and Neglect Data System: Table 2-1: Screened-In and Screened-Out Referrals, pg 25, https://www.acf.hhs.gov/sites/default/files/cb/cm2016.pdf (2016).

6. U.S. Department of Health and Human Services, Administration for Children and Families, Administration on Children, Youth and Families, Children's Bureau. (2018). Child Maltreatment 2016: Report from the States to the National Child Abuse and Neglect Data System: Table 3-3: Child Victims, pg 47, https://www.acf.hhs.gov/sites/default/files/cb/cm2016.pdf (2016).

7. National Law Center on Homelessness & Poverty, TENT CITY, USA: The Growth of America's Homeless Encampments and How Communities are Responding, https://www.nlchp.org/Tent_City_USA_2017 (2017)

8. Semega, J; Fotenot, KR; Kollar, MA., "Income and Poverty in the United States: 2016." Census Bureau, https://www.census.gov/library/publications/2017/demo/p60-259.html (September 2017).

9. The National Low Income Housing Coalition, THE GAP: The Affordable Housing Gap Analysis 2016, http://nlihc.org/sites/default/files/Gap-Report_2017.pdf, (March 2017)

10. Joint Center for Housing Studies of Harvard University, The State of the Nation's Housing, http://www.jchs.harvard.edu/sites/default/files/harvard_jchs_state_of_the_nations_housing_2017_0.pdf, (2017).

11. Beck Hughes, Working Homeless Population Grows in Cities Throughout the US., Parade Magazine, https://parade.com/643064/beckyhughes/working-homeless-population-grows-in-cities-across-the-u-s/ (February 2018).

12. John Schmitt and Kris Warner, "Ex-offenders and the Labor Market," Center for Economic and Policy Research, http://cepr.net/documents/publications/ex-offenders-2010-11.pdf, (November 2010).

13. National Coalition for the Homeless, Substance Abuse and Homelessness, https://www.nationalhomeless.org/factsheets/addiction.pdf (July 2009).

14. Didenko & Pankratz, "Substance use: Pathways to homelessness? or a way of adapting to street life?," National Mental Health Association, (January 2006).

15. Fisher, G. L., & Roget, N. A. (Eds.). "Encyclopedia of substance abuse prevention, treatment, and recovery." SAGE Publications, Inc. (2009).

16. Caroline Crosson Gilpin, "Should People Give Money to Panhandlers?," The New York Times, https://www.nytimes.com/2017/03/07/learning/should-people-give-money-to-panhandlers.html, (March 7, 2017).

17. John Harper, "Akron's debt approaching $1 billion: What does that mean?" Cleveland. com, https://www.cleveland.com/akron/index.ssf/2015/09/akrons_debt_approaching_1_bill.html (September 22, 2015).

18. American Civil Liberties Union of Washington, "Anti-Panhandling Laws – Important Case Law and Frequently Asked Questions," file:///home/chronos/u-fa68dd5c-c37ae1d01ff2f61a3e8c47183169d5ff/Downloads/legal_primer_-_panhandling%20(1). pdf, (2016)

19. The 2016 Annual Homeless Assessment Report (AHAR) to Congress, Part 1: Point-in-Time Estimates of Homelness, https://www.hudexchange.info/resources/documents/2016-AHAR-Part-1.pdf, (November 2016).

20. Samantha Raphelson, "How The Loss Of U.S. Psychiatric Hospitals Led To A Mental Health Crisis," National Public Radio, https://www.npr.org/2017/11/30/567477160/how-the-loss-of-u-s-psychiatric-hospitals-led-to-a-mental-health-crisis, (November 30, 2017).

21. Greenberg, G. A., & Rosenheck, R. A., "Jail incarceration, homelessness, and mental health: A national study," Psychiatric Services, https://www.ncbi.nlm.nih.gov/pubmed/18245159, (2009).

22. Steven Raphael and Michael A. Stoll , "Assessing the Contribution of the Deinstitutionalization of the Mentally Ill to Growth in the U.S. Incarceration Rate" The Journal of Legal Studies, The University of Chicago Press, https://gspp.berkeley.edu/assets/uploads/research/pdf/p71.pdf, (January 2013).

23. Kirk Johnson, "A Homeless Camp in Our Back Yard? Please, a University Says," The New York Times, https://www.nytimes.com/2018/02/27/us/homeless-camp-seattle.html, (February 27, 2018).

24. City of Seattle, Homeless Response/ City-Permitted Villages, https://www.seattle.gov/homelessness/city-permitted-villages, (2018).

25. Hope Village Las Cruces | Off of the Streets and Closer to a Home, https://hopevillage-

lascruces.wordpress.com/ (2018)

26. SquareOne Villages | Opportunity Village, https://www.squareonevillages.org/opportunity, (2018)

27. Community First! Village | Mobile Loaves & Fishes, https://mlf.org/community-first/, (2018)

28. National Law Center on Homelessness & Poverty, TENT CITY, USA: The Growth of America's Homeless Encampments and How Communities are Responding, https://www.nlchp.org/Tent_City_USA_2017 (2017)

29. Ohio.com, Opinion, "Mar-Quetta Boddie, Rebecca Callahan, Keith Stahl and Fred Berry: Second Chance Village is not a solution to homelessness, https://www.ohio.com/akron/editorial/mar-quetta-boddie-rebecca-callahan-ken-stahl-and-fred-berry-second-chance-village-is-not-a-solution-to-homelessness, (July 11, 2018)

30. U.S. Department of Housing and Urban Development Office of Policy Development and Research, Costs Associated With First-Time Homelessness for Families and Individuals, https://www.huduser.gov/publications/pdf/costs_homeless.pdf, (MArch, 2010)

31. Susan Scutti, "CDC committee recommends routine hepatitis A vaccination for homeless people," https://www.cnn.com/2018/10/24/health/hepatitis-a-vaccine-homeless-cdc/index.html, (October 24, 2018).

32. National Alliance to End Homelessness, Ending Chronic Homelessness Saves Taxpayers Money, https://endhomelessness.org/resource/ending-chronic-homelessness-saves-taxpayers-money/ (November 6, 2015).

Made in the USA
Columbia, SC
15 April 2019